V. M. J. Viljanen

About Freemasonry
in Finland and Russia

Collectanea Masonica Paperback Series no. 1

ORIGINAL TEXT: VAPAAMUURARIUDESTA SUOMESSA JA VENÄJÄLLÄ, 1923

ISBN 978-952-65251-3-6 (SOFTCOVER)
ISBN 978-952-65251-4-3 (PDF)
ISBN 978-952-65251-5-0 (EPUB)

Dedicated to
The Grand Lodge of New York State
and its
Most Worshipful
Grand Master
Arthur S. Tompkins

Grand Master of the Grand Lodge of of New-York State
Judge Arthur S. Tompkins.

FOREWORD

This booklet, probably the first in the Finnish language to deal with real Freemasonry, is primarily intended for Masons on this side of the Atlantic and the other side: as a short, modest guide to the treasures of old historical memories and as a grateful mention of the work that American Freemasonry, and especially The Grand Lodge of New York State, has done to revive Freemasonry in Finland. At the same time, it should also arouse interest in those non-Masonic circles who are generally interested in learning about the Masonic movement and its earlier history in our own country and in Russia, as well as its rebirth in independent Finland.

The section on Russian Freemasonry has been included in the book because when Finland came under Russian rule, Freemasonry in both countries suffered the same fate, and many historical aspects of Finland and Russia are illuminated by it.

As the contents of the book are mainly confined to the framework of an earlier lecture, it is rather limited. Those who need more information will find it in the bibliography at the end of the book. No doubt he will then also find the answer to his question: what is Freemasonry?

Helsinki, 12 October 1923.

Author.

I

THE BIRTH OF MODERN FREEMASONRY

> Motto: "Freemasonry is and wants to be
> free in the highest sense of the word
> and noblest sense".
>
> King Oscar II.

The chronicles tell us that on St. John's Day, i.e. Midsummer's Day, 1717, the members of four Masonic Lodges then operating in London met and decided to form a Grand Lodge and elected a Grand Master or Grand Lordship to lead it.

Six years later, in 1723, this Grand Lodge issued a special publication — the Constitutions — which, in addition to the history of Freemasonry, etc., contained the rules under which the Lodges and Masons were to operate.

This year — 1923 — marks the two hundredth anniversary of the date on which this publication laid the foundations of the Masonic organisation as we know it today.

The Masonic movement had existed before, but in a different form. As such, its history goes back a long way — to the time of the Egyptian pharaohs, according to some scholars.

Reorganised from London, Freemasonry began to gain ground and spread throughout the world. Remarkably, it inspired all classes of people, from the ancient nobility to the clergy. Famous names from all walks of life can be found on its membership lists, both then and later.

Freemasonry had become an international organisation. In this sense, it is the oldest of its kind.

EARLIER FREEMASONRY IN FINLAND

Freemasonry came to Finland from the then mother country, Sweden, whose capital, Stockholm, had already established a Masonic lodge in 1735.

From there, under the patronage of the elected hereditary prince *Adolf Fredrik*, the movement spread to Finland, where a lodge was founded in the capital, Turku, in 1756 under the name "Pyhä Johannes-loosi Augustin" (St. John's Lodge of Augustin).

The lodge was probably named after *Augustin Ehrensvärd*, the famous builder of Viapori — now Suomenlinna — who was a high-ranking Swedish Mason.

Of naturally, the Lodge was run under the Swedish system as it was part of the Stockholm Land Lodge at the time.

Another lodge called "Stuart" is said to have been active in Turku at the same time. However, there is very little information about it. Judging by its name, it was a Masonic lodge of the highest degree, known as a chapter.

The first Master of Augustin Lodge was *John Jennings*, a Master of Horsemanship and Lord Chamberlain. He was a member of the Swedish Parliament. Therefore, when he was in Stockholm in 1762, he also held lodge meetings there.

In the same year, the lodge was ordered to move to Helsinki and the then Governor of Uusimaa and Hämeenlääni, Baron *Boije*, was appointed Master. With such a high level of protection, it is not surprising that the lodge was allowed to hold its meetings in the old town hall, by order of the magistrate.

Even after this, lodge meetings were held alternately in Helsinki and Stockholm. The last residence in Helsinki was a wooden house on the site of the present Knights' Hall.

When Finland came under Russian rule, the number of members of the Augustini Lodge was 460. After the separation from the motherland, the activities of the Lodge gradually diminished and the Lodge ceased to exist in 1813.

Surviving membership lists show that the lodge's masters and officers were mainly high-ranking military officers, including the King's Adjutant General. The names of doctors and priests also appear in the lists.

In 1777 — the year after "Grand Master *Elagin* of all Russian Freemasons" suddenly changed the Masonic lodges in Russia to the German-Swedish system — a new lodge was founded in Helsinki under the name of "Phoenix".

It had actually been founded in Stockholm in 1767. The Stockholm Lodge was started by *Tullmann*, the secretary of the English Embassy in Stockholm, who had been authorised by the London Grand Lodge.

Naturally, the Stockholm grand lodge would not tolerate the intrusion of a foreign grand lodge into its territory. A bitter dispute ensued between the dubious Tullmann and the Stockholm Grand Lodge. To make matters worse, London could not help Tullmann either, as the Phoenix Lodge ceased to exist. Or rather, it was merged with the two Andreas Lodges because, as the documents explain, "circumstances demanded that the Andreas Lodge should be established in Finland, and as Brother *Biörnberg* has already been elected Master of this Lodge, it is named Phoenix, so that by the merger this name would not be lost from Swedish Masonic history and so that the decorations and equipments belonging to the Lodge could follow the name".

The same Biörnberg, who later became a Major in Loviisa, had essentially received his Masonic degree in France. He went on to become Master of both Augustine and Phoenix Lodges.

Although information on Masonic activities in Finland is scarce, the surviving documents give the impression that they had a significant impact on our cultural and social life at the time. And there was no shortage of opponents. There is one case from that period when opposition came to the fore in a very serious way. When *Zacharias Cajander*, then vicar of Helsinki, was elected to the Swedish Parliament by the diocesan consistory, he was accused of being a Freemason and therefore unfit to be a representative. Moreover, he had been elected by the votes of his relative *Forthelius*. However, the consistory did not take this into account and Mr Cajander's election was confirmed.

Some of the decorations and signs used by the Freemasons of the time have been preserved in the Turku Historical Museum and our National Museum. Of particular interest are the aprons and chain collars. They should be brought to the attention of freemason researchers and studied in the archives of the Grand Lodge of Stockholm. The information in the museums is very incomplete and undoubtedly partly incorrect. Our historical research would also benefit greatly from such work. It is not known with certainty where the documents and archives of the lodges have gone. Perhaps such a study would help to clarify this too.

It may be mentioned in this connection that both lodges in Finland celebrated their feast day as Charles Day, i.e. 28 January. This was due to the accession of Duke *Carl of Södermanland* — later King *Carl XIII* of Sweden — to the leadership of Swedish Freemasonry in 1774. Since then, the names of male members of the Swedish monarchy and royal house have appeared on the Masonic rolls.

SECRET SOCIETIES DURING SWEDISH RULE

Until now it has been very difficult to determine to what extent the many secret societies that were active in our country during the 17th century and the first half of the following century were of Masonic origin. Although there are references to them in our historical literature, it is likely that they were only fraternities of the Masonic type. They still exist today all over the world. True Freemasons do not accept them into their organisation.

The most famous of these was the "Valhalla" brotherhood in Viapori — now Suomenlinna — whose aim was supposedly 'to celebrate the history of the fatherland'. In reality, this was probably not the only purpose of its activities, since according to surviving documents, several of its 313 members were among the executors of the Anjala conspiracy, which has become notorious in our history. The "Valhalla" also had subdivisions. As such, I mention the 'Pyhän Akselin maja' (St Aksel's Hut) in Turku.

The "Valhalla" was dissolved or ceased to exist in 1786. It is noteworthy that in the same year a new brotherhood was founded in Loviisa under the name of "Amore proximi'. Its members were mainly military men from the local fortress of Svartholm. The list of members of this society bears the autograph of *Henrik Gabriel Porthan*. Other prominent members were *P. af Enehjelm, Baron B. Stackelberg* and *Mauri Klingspor*. Of these, Baron Stackelberg is known as a supporter of the ideas of *Yrjö Maunu Sprengtporten*, the advocate of Finnish independence.

It is highly probable that Sprengtporten was the soul behind the founding of Amore Proximi, although he wished to remain secret, just as he undoubtedly worked invisibly in the Valhalla Brotherhood. The fact that these and many other similar societies pursued aims alien to the Empire and were not genuine Masonic societies is demonstrated by the fact that, in 1803, King *Gustav IV Adolf* issued a decree requiring all societies operating in the Empire to submit their rules for examination and confirmation.

The decree explicitly stated that the measure did not apply to "Masonic lodges under the protection of the king" — it is worth noting that the current king and heir to the Swedish throne is also a member of the Masonic order.

After this, a large number of societies disappeared from our country. The "Amore proximi" is known to have ceased to exist in 1813. Whether it submitted its rules for approval and received permission to continue its activities is not clear. No doubt the archives of the Grand Lodge of Stockholm could provide an explanation for this, as well as for its activities in general.

THE MOST FAMOUS FREEMASONS IN FINLAND

AUGUSTIN EHRENSVÄRD

In Suomenlinna Castle, under a beautiful memorial stone carved by Sergel, decorated with a bronze-cast gunboat cock and stern bow and surmounted by a warrior's shield, helmet and sword, lies "in the midst of his work and his fleet" — as the memorial reads — Field Marshal Count *Augustin Ehrensvärd.*

It has been called a fortunate coincidence that, despite the bombing, the tombstone of the castle's founder has remained intact, just as it was placed there two hundred years ago. It is also to the credit of the Russians, who later occupied the fortress, that they left Ehrensvärd's grave intact for independent Finland.

Augustin Ehrensvärd was actually of Finnish origin, as his father *Juhana Jaakko Schäffer,* who was ennobled as Ehrensvärd, was a native of Finland. Augustin himself was born and brought up in Sweden in 1710. This he developed through his extensive travels abroad. His hobby was not purely military, but military-technical-scientific.

Ehrensvärd first came to Finland in 1747 as a member of the Secret Defence Commission. He visited several places to find a suitable central fortress for the defence of Finland. He finally settled on the Susi Islands off Helsinki. It was decided to build the fortress according to Ehrensväld's proposal and in 1750 it was named Sveaborg, also at Ehrensväld's suggestion.

Ehrensvärd dedicated his life's work to the restoration of this famous fortress and its associated archipelago fleet. Except for a short period, he was in charge of this major project for almost 24 years until his death.

Through this great work, Ehrensvärd has forever etched his name in the pages of our country's history. Although his plans and constructions no longer have the same military and technical

Augustin Ehrensvärd

significance as they once did, it is gratifying to note that they were nevertheless fundamental to the defence system now entrusted to the men of independent Finland.

The Finnish Ehrensvärd became the pioneer of free Finnish maritime rescue.

Very little is known about Ehrensvärd's Masonic activities in our country. He was undoubtedly one of the highest ranking Freemasons in Sweden, as the first lodge founded in Finland — Augustin — was named after him.

He has an honorable place in Masonic history and his memory will never fade.

His admirable industry and energy, his great loyalty and honesty will always remain an example to the Masons of our country.

FREDRIK GRANATENHJELM

On a lonely hill in the northern corner of Kaisaniemi Park, not far from the shore of Töölönlahti Bay, stands a burial mound known as the Masonic Tomb, whose only decoration until recently was a multi-edged granite boulder that had fallen to the ground.

Now the top of the mound has been lined with smooth-edged kerbstones and the sunken monument has been raised. The words can be read: "Likagodt om världen vet, hvem här h(v)ilar, Gud vet hvar han gjort och uslingen välsingnar hans minne" (Whether the world knows who rests here, God knows what he has done, and the unfortunate bless his memory).

The above words are a very fitting description of the outlook and character of the man whose resting place is spoken of.

The man's name was *Fredrik Granatenhjelm*; he was a major by rank and the former owner of the present Kaisaniemi Park, the University Botanical Gardens and the surrounding areas.

Granatenhjelm was a Swedish citizen and a member of the Swedish army. When Ehrensvärd started building Suomenlinna, Granatenhjelm was moved to the castle hill there. As a Freemason, he was a friend of Ehrensvärd.

As a deeply religious and honest man, nothing could have led him to become involved in the political conflicts that characterised this period in the history of the Swedish kingdom.

As evidence of Granatenhjelm's state of mind, the following historical story is known.

When *Jaakko Maunu Sprengtporten*, Yrjö Maunu Sprengtporten's half-brother, suddenly stormed the castle at Suomenlinna and swore his officers and soldiers to loyalty and obedience to King Gustav III, who had staged a coup d'état, Granatenhjelm refused to take the oath. His conscience, he said, would not allow him to break the oath he had just sworn to the king and the nobles. The new oath was therefore

The grave of Fredrik Granatenhjelm in Kaisaniemi.

not taken, and Sprengtporten was satisfied with the answer he had received, which he accepted by embracing Granatenhjelm.

As his anonymous obituary indicates, Granatenhjelm was a philanthropist in every sense of the word. He founded and ran schools for poor soldiers' children and was an unknown help to many.

When Granatenhjelm died at the age of 76, the Masonic community of the time escorted him with great ceremony to his current resting place in Kaisaniemi. He had chosen it himself. For a long time, the people of Helsinki talked about this as a remarkable event.

ABOLITION OF MASONIC LODGES IN FINLAND

When Finland came under Russian rule in 1809, ties with the former motherland were severed and Masonic activity could no longer flourish in the new circumstances. In 1813, the Phoenix and Augustin Lodges closed their doors, and after that there were no real Masonic Lodges in Finland.

The death blow to the movement in our country came from Emperor *Alexander I.* On 1 August 1822, he issued a decree ordering the abolition of all Masonic fraternities and secret societies throughout the Russian Empire. Four years later, Emperor *Nicholas I* renewed this decree, stating that every civil servant in Finland should give a written undertaking to renounce such societies, whether domestic or foreign. The order concerning the University of Turku includes the names of *Robert Rehbinder* and *Carl Gustaf Mannerheim*. The decree concerning the Turku Court of Appeal and other offices is printed in the Collection of Finnish Decrees.

There is no doubt that this regulation was followed as far as the country's civil service was concerned. Instead, contact with foreign lodges was maintained through those who, as free traders, had the opportunity to visit outside the country's borders. As far as the Swedish lodges were concerned, such contact would have existed throughout the Russian period. Similarly, our sea captains seem to have been generally members of English Masonic lodges.

Our emigrants and those in America, on the other hand, came into contact with Masonic lodges in the United States, where they were very well supported and active. Incidentally, a lodge was founded in Philadelphia quite early, in 1731 — earlier than in Scandinavian countries, for example — and the famous statesman Benjamin Franklin was once Grand Master of one of the Masonic lodges there. The founder of the United States of America and its first President, *George Washington*, was also a Freemason. He was a member of St John's Lodge in New York State. He took his in-

George Washington takes the oath of presidency at the St. John's Lodge bible.

auguration oath on the Bible of this Lodge — which, incidentally, still exists. Our picture shows the occasion. So did the recently deceased President of the United States. *Warren S. Harding* belonged to a Masonic lodge in the state of Ohio. He too took his oath of his presidential office on the same Bible.

Undoubtedly, the benefits obtained in this way — through contact with the Freemasons of the world — by private citizens, without public knowledge, in the defence of the rights of our country and in the defence and preservation of our national liberation, cannot be underestimated. Freemasons, who number in the millions and are spread all over the world, also took part in this work.

THE REVIVAL OF FREEMASONRY IN FINLAND

It was only natural that the idea of reviving Freemasonry in Finland should have arisen as soon as Finland had the opportunity to throw off its centuries-old shackles and become an independent country.

However, neither the economic turmoil caused by the war and the rebellion, nor the less confused state of affairs delayed the realisation of the idea until 1921, when, with the help of the Grand Lodge of New York, a Masonic lodge was founded in the capital of Finland under the name of Suomi Loosi I (Finland Lodge I). It is noteworthy that it was founded with the help of America, the most powerful power in the world, both politically and economically, and exactly 150 years after the death of Augustin Ehrensvärd, Finland's most famous Freemason.

Thus, after almost exactly 100 years of stagnation, Freemasonry has been revived in our country. It is now the duty of those who have entered the books of the new lodge to develop the Masonic spirit in Finland that they inherited centuries ago.

Thanks to the enthusiasm of the members of the Grand Lodge of New York and the Finnish Lodge, the work has been so successful that a lodge has been established in Tampere — whose name has now appeared for the first time in the pages of Masonic history — and the former Phoenix Lodge has been revived in Turku. Sooner or later, these lodges will be able to establish the first free Grand Lodge in Finland, and thus come into contact and cooperation with other lodges of equal status throughout the world. Interaction with them will probably strengthen the international position of our country and will be a blessing for our country and for all mankind.

In the first half of the same year, a lodge called St. Augustin was established in Helsinki with the help of the Grand Lodge of Stockholm. We hope that cooperation with this lodge will be mutually beneficial and fruitful.

OFFICIAL REPORT ON THE RESTORATION OF FREEMASONRY IN FINLAND

(Extract from the annual report of Grand Master Arthur S. Tompkins
of the New-York State Grand Lodge, 1 May 1923).

After the last Grand Lodge (1922), a group of Masonic brethren initiated in America and now living in Finland sent us a petition requesting a charter for the re-establishment of a new Masonic Lodge in the city of Helsinki, Finland.

After careful consideration, the Grand Master (Most Worshipful *Arthur S. Tompkins*[1]), on the basis of the Grand Lodge Warrant of 1921 (to establish a Lodge in the Free Territories), decided to grant the requested charter and establish the Lodge, appointing the former Master of Gorruwood Lodge No. 569, Brooklyn, Finland, who is a native of Finland, Most Worshipful Brother T. T. Nekton, as Deputy Grand Master. H. Nekton as Deputy Grand Master of the Masonic District of the Republic of Finland. Equipped with a temporary warrant and our instructions, he travelled to Finland before the arrival of the Grand Master to make the necessary preparations for the initiation of the Lodge in question.

Last August (1922), the Grand Master travelled to Finland accompanied by a commission appointed by the Grand Lodge to investigate the Masonic situation in Europe, consisting of the Most Worshipful *Townsend Scudder*, the Most Worshipful *Robert J. Kenworthy* and the Most Worshipful *Ossian Lang*. I will say more about the work of this Commission later.

On our arrival in Helsinki everything was in perfect order for the inauguration of the new Lodge.

More than a hundred years earlier, the Russians had expelled Freemasonry from Finland and confiscated Masonic proper-

---

1 Mr Arthur S. Tompkins is a Justice of the Supreme Court of the State of New York and Chairman of the Judiciary Committee of the local county.

Benjamin Franklin as Grand Master of the Grand Lodge of Pennsylvania.

ty; now that the war was over and the Republic of Finland was established, the idea arose among Masons living in Finland and others who wished to join our fraternity to ask the Grand Lodge of New-York to re-establish Freemasonry in Finland. In the old Parliament House in Helsinki, where the same Russian power that had driven Freemasonry out of the country had once conducted the affairs of state, we saw a large hall converted into a perfectly arranged Masonic Lodge, with its furniture, tools and symbols; here we initiated into the Third Degree about forty good Finnish citizens who had been admitted to membership in the Lodge, which had previously been operating under a temporary licence granted by us.

They were all highly educated men, and most of them spoke English, so the work was done in that language. On the same day, after the installation work, this new Lodge, Suomi Loosi I, was inaugurated as usual, and its officers were solemnly installed. All the ceremonies were presided over by the Grand Master, assisted by Brothers Scudder and Kenworthy, Lang and Nekton, and at the consecration of the Lodge also by Brother James Kilby, a member of Rockland Lodge No. 723.

The character of this new Lodge is illustrated by its founder members, the great majority of whom were men in leading positions in the economic, political, commercial and business life of the Republic of Finland. — — —

They expressed their gratitude in a letter received by our Grand Secretary last November (1922), from which we quote as follows:

"America has had the opportunity to be of great and varied assistance to beleaguered nations throughout the world at this time of trial. Its "power state" of New York has always borne the brunt of these far-reaching measures.

As a further example of this benevolence and generosity, we note with sincerity and gratitude that the Most Worshipful Fraternity of New-York State has brought us the firm bonds of Masonic principles and has indelibly united them among our people.

The expedition of your Most Worshipful Grand Master, Arthur S. Tompkins, and his officers, K. K. Robert Judson Kenworthy, K. K. Townsend Scudder, T. K. Ossian Lang, and T. K. Hope H. Nekton, to our country, and their donation to the endowment of our first Lodge, is a noble sacrifice, which cannot be materially repaid to a Grand Lodge so worthy as this worthy Fraternity. We have already tried to express our inner feelings to these good Brethren in person. We now wish to express to your Most Worshipful Grand Lodge all the deep respect and gratitude which fills the hearts of all our brethren, and with which our own Finnish Masonry will warm the bosoms of the people.

Whether we shall be able to fully discharge the great duty entrusted to us, the future will show. But, as you have freely and voluntarily given us this opportunity, we also sincerely pledge ourselves to do our utmost to promote worthily the noble work which you have entrusted to us, and to spread its blessed spirit in our part of the country, so that your Most Worshipful Grand Lodge may be honoured and we may enjoy and benefit from it.

With the deepest gratitude we draw, — — etc.

Since then, we have received an application for a charter from another lodge to be established in Tampere. The application was unanimously supported by the entire membership of Suomi Loosi I. The application was approved. The Tampere Lodge was granted a Charter. The lodge will be established by the Finnish Deputy Grand Master or any other Deputy Commissioner appointed by the Grand Master.

It has also recently come to our attention that a third application has been received from Finland. If this is also accepted and this Lodge is formed, the necessary number of local Lodges will be found to form a Grand Lodge in Finland. It is very gratifying to note that our Grand Lodge has had the opportunity to revive Freemasonry in Finland and to place it on such a firm and solid foundation.

We were assured in Helsinki that Freemasonry would spread throughout the country and become a great national and moral force in Finland.

II

THE FORMER FREEMASONRY IN RUSSIA

It took more than half a century after the founding of the London Grand Lodge for Freemasonry in its present form — as defined in the movement's charter — to gain a foothold in Russia.

All sorts of movements and endeavours close to Freemasonry — often mislabelled as such — with the intention of inducing people to good works and obedience, had already existed there and had prepared the ground for it. The most notable of these were the 'Rosicrucians', whose origins are still obscure. The most popular theory is that they originated with the German nobleman *Christian Rosenkreuz,* who had travelled to the East.

Another movement that gained support in Russia, particularly in the Baltic provinces, was known as the 'Strikte Observanz' (Strict Observance) and is thought to have been a continuation of the Knights Templar, which had ceased to exist centuries earlier.

Instead, the actual Freemasonry of the London Charter — self-styled Free and Right — did not appear in Russia until 1771. In that year, the academic director of an aristocratic country school for cadets, the German *von Reichell,* founded a Masonic lodge in St Petersburg under the name of 'Apollo'. The founding members — with the exception of a Russian general — were Germans.

Apollo Lodge was licensed and operated by the Berlin Grand Landlodge, which was already operating from Berlin at the time. It was undoubtedly from their origins, or at least their contribution, that it was born.

Apollo Lodge had barely got off the ground when a new lodge called "Perfect Unanimity" appeared in St Petersburg to compete with it. It had received its mandate from the London Grand Lodge. Both refused to co-operate with Apollo Lodge, and the London Grand Lodge declared that it alone had the exclusive right to establish Masonic Lodges in the world. Before discussions with Berlin could reach any stage, London appointed a Russian Privy Councillor, Senator and member of the Imperial Cabinet, *Elagin,* as they said, "Grand Master of all Russians".

Berlin gave in and the Apollo Lodge closed its doors. Such was the power of the London Grand Lodge in the Masonic world at that time.

But von Reichell, the founder of Apollo, did not remain inactive. In 1773, he was reunited with the Russian Prince *Trubetskoy* in his efforts to found the Lodge. The lodge was named 'Harpokrates'. In the same year, he founded three more lodges in St Petersburg. The former Apollo also became active again, founding a brother lodge of the same name in Riga and a lodge called 'Isis' in Tallinn.

There is every reason to believe that von Reichell had the support, or at least the sympathy, of the Grand Lodge of Berlin. He also had the unusual support of his friend, the Russian Prince Trubetskoi, with whom he had founded the 'Osiris' Lodge in Moscow. This was commonly known as the "Prince's Lodge" because most of its members were princes, or at least nobles.

Naturally, the Masonic work initiated by the English did not fail. Soon there were three lodges in St Petersburg, plus one in Moscow and a Military Lodge in Yassy, made up entirely of military personnel.

The Moscow lodge was called "Muse-Clio". This feminine name is said to derive from its relationship with the then Russian Empress *Catherine II.* She had become its guardian spirit.

The two Masonic systems of the time, the English, represented by the Grand Lodge of London, and the German Berlin Masonic Lodge — which is said to have taken over its programme of activities from the Stockholm Masonic Association in 1759 — had thus gained a significant foothold in Russia. It should be added that there was no question of cooperation between them. The Grand Lodge of London consistently maintained its position that the German Grand Lodge of Berlin had no right to engage in Masonic work in Russia. The "dispute over Russia" between the future Great Powers therefore already existed at that time.

Now there was a rather remarkable turn of events. All in all, it was due to the motives of the Great Powers.

Catherine's policy at this time required the cooperation of the then *King Gustav III* of Sweden and *King Frederick II* of Prussia. Relations with the former were maintained by Catherine's favourite, the *Count of Panin*, who was minister to Russia at the Swedish court. He was a Freemason and very enthusiastic about the Swedish Masonic system. When Frederick II — who, incidentally, had become a Freemason in 1738, when he was already heir to the throne — declared the Berlin Masonic Lodge to be under his patronage in 1774, it was natural that these two Grand Lodges — Stockholm and Berlin — should maintain lively contact with each other. Catherine took advantage of this in her policies, especially as she began to develop a dislike for all things English after realising the growing importance of England in the quest for world domination.

Naturally, she 'ordered' Elagin, the English-appointed 'Grand Master of all Russian Freemasons', to bring his lodges into line with the Swedish-German system. As a courtier dependent on his mistress, Elagin also immediately made a turnaround.

All freemason lodges in Russia became subject to the Berlin regulations.

Germanism had won a great victory in Russia.

London had lost its cause for the time being.

This happened in the year of grace, 1776.

NEW DEVELOPMENTS AND SURPRISES

All lodges in Russia were united under a provincial lodge, now established in St Petersburg, which in 1777 included 18 Masonic lodges. Of these, 10 were in St Petersburg, 3 in Moscow, Tallinn, Arkhangelsk and Polotsk, and there was also the military lodge mentioned above. Count von Panin and Prince *Gagarin* are the first names to appear in the membership lists.

However, there was a major distraction. It was done without a warrant. The Berlin Masonic Lodge had no right to grant one, and the London Grand Lodge, which still had full power in the Masonic world, naturally did not. The basis for action was therefore weak. In the absence of legality, it was difficult to maintain cooperation and discipline between lodges.

The consequences soon became apparent. Although the documents and information from this period are rather incomplete, it is clear that the split that soon followed was mainly caused by a mixed-race man named *von Rosenberg* and the Russian nationalism that was already taking hold at that time.

At that time, the aforementioned von Rosenberg, a military adventurer and globetrotter who had participated in the Seven Years' War and was fluent in several languages, was the Worshipful Master of Apollo, the first Masonic lodge to be established in Russia. It was characteristic of this man that he had once fought for and against France. With the help of his friend, the Russian Prince *Kurokin*, who was ambassador to the Swedish court, he began to maintain relations with the Grand Lodge in Stockholm. These relations became so friendly that when King Gustav III made a trip to St. Petersburg, von Rosenberg was able to persuade him to pay a courtesy visit to his lodge in Apollo. His goal of gaining the recognition and patronage of the Grand Lodge of Sweden for his lodge was achieved after the King's brother, the Duke of Södermanland — later King Carl XIII — gave his consent. The year was 1779. Apollo and three other

George Washington as a Freemason at a lodge event for orphaned children.

lodges in St. Petersburg, Kronstadt and Tallinn formed their own Swedish Provincial Lodge under the leadership of Prince Gagarin.

Sweden was thus also involved in the struggle for Masonic supremacy in Russia. But London was not idle. In fact, the aforementioned Elagin maintained constant relations with the London Grand Lodge. When Apollo and Kastor in Riga and Pollux in Tartu, the two Baltic Lodges, were about to form their own provincial Grand Lodges and merge with the Berlin Grand Lodge, Elagin managed to intervene and bring them under London's control as Grand Lodges — that is, to operate under the English system.

This was a very serious blow to Germanism in the Baltic countries, as the Masonic lodges represented the civilized classes in these countries and carried on cultural work in the German spirit. The German sources of the time consider the conversion of these forerunners to the other spirit as a ruthless crime.

This happened in 1785.

The Russian Osiris Lodge in Moscow had also begun to show signs of dissent. This lodge included the Moscow nobility of the time, up to and including the court. Since only the elected nobility could become members of the Lodge, of which the aforementioned Prince Trubetskoy was the ruler, it was generally known as the "Prince's Lodge," as mentioned above. Trubetskoy was sympathetic to German aspirations, but could not resist the growing movement: Russia for Russians in Freemasonry. Osiris used to declare itself an independent Russian Landlodge.

Thus, before the end of the 1700s, there were three more or less nationally alien Masonic movements and organizations in Russia: the Provincial Lodge under the Grand Lodge of London, headed by the former Elagin, the Provincial Lodge under the Grand Lodge of Stockholm, headed by Prince Gagarin, and the Russian Land Lodge, headed by Prince Trubetskoi. The first two were based in St. Petersburg, the third in Moscow.

All three systems were in full swing. Lodges were established throughout the Russian Empire. The Swedes seem to have been the most successful. They had influence in 17 lodges, 9 of which were based in St. Petersburg. The languages used were Russian and German.

The English, on the other hand, had taken over mainly the Baltic countries, except for the capital, St. Petersburg. They ran three lodges in the capital itself and 10 elsewhere.

The Russian Landlodge seems to have had the least success. It included only two lodges in Moscow and one in Riga.

Berlin had completely lost its ability to function and, at the same time, its influence in the Russian Masonic world. There is also no doubt that its influence on Russian political and cultural life had diminished considerably at the same time. The fact that Elagin, who had been Catherine's humble servant, had the courage to change his position and work for London was undoubtedly due to Catherine's changed relationship with Freemasonry, or perhaps vice versa. Believing it to be a revolutionary movement, Catherine was only waiting for an opportunity to attack it.

FREEMASONRY AND CATHERINE II

It was natural that the rival and more or less alien currents competing with Freemasonry for power in Russia should have a very harmful effect on Freemasonry as such. The members of the lodges were of different nationalities, different in spirit, language and customs. The competition between lodges in different circles naturally brought into the lodges elements that had other purposes than Freemasonry itself. Moreover, when becoming a Freemason became fashionable in many circles and membership became easy, it is understandable that lodge activity did not become what it should have been: internal construction became a side issue among other aspirations. This was likely to cause resentment and dissension in serious and truly Masonic circles.

This was the subject of gossip in Catherine's ears. She was more than happy to hear it. Her literary instincts were stimulated, and she began to mock and whip her contemporaries, especially the Freemasons, in the form of satirical plays. According to Catherine — who was not without reason called a later manifestation of the Venusian Emperor Nero — the Freemasons were "people who made gold, sold the elixir of life and were fortune-tellers". Even Catherine's knowledge of the Freemasons was rather sketchy and inaccurate, as, strangely enough, is the case with many even today. Had she taken the trouble to inform herself before taking up her pen, she would have had the opportunity, like everyone else, to learn that Freemasonry is founded on the noble ideals of humanity and morality. Moreover, she made the mistake, like many others before and after her, of confusing "free and legitimate Freemasonry" with all sorts of mysterious movements with which it has nothing to do.

Undoubtedly, the main purpose of Catherine's literary attacks was to weaken the foundations of Freemasonry in Russia so that she could more easily crush it with her mighty hand. It should be remembered that the Masonic lodges of the time had members from very influential circles, including the court. Among them were her son *Paul* and the then famous writer and socialite *N.I. Novikoff*, who in his satirical writings had ridiculed the civil service and excessive French admiration. It was therefore necessary first to discredit the whole movement as such. Undoubtedly, Catherine was also motivated by vanity, since as a woman she could not become a member of a real Masonic lodge. In addition, with the French Revolution raging at the time — which, incidentally, was allegedly carried out by Freemasons — she thought it best to first have Novikoff imprisoned and then, a few years later, to declare the lodge outlawed. This order probably came to the lodges in the form of a "wish" from the Empire.

This was in 1794.

However Catherine the Great may have been judged as a human being, the revival of the sciences and the arts, the elevation of civilization and the improvement of the health of the people were the most important points of her endeavors. It thus pursued essentially the same ideals as Freemasonry.

These are the words of a German Masonic writer on Russian Freemasonry.

The Russian literary historian *Petrov* — who, incidentally, had nothing to do with Freemasonry — cites the awakening of Russian nationalism and the spread of Freemasonry as a counterweight to the French philosophy of life in Russia.

Russian Freemasonry had thus passed through its first phase, which lasted only 23 years.

THE LATER STAGES OF RUSSIAN FREEMASONRY

Two years later Catherine II died. Her mentally weak son Paul I, a Freemason, succeeded her on the Russian throne.

One would have expected that the Masonic movement would be allowed to operate again in Russia.

However, things went in the opposite direction.

Napoleon harassed the Knights of Malta, and they turned to Paul I in their distress. He was informed that, in return for his help, he would receive this famous Mediterranean island under his protection.

Paul was very pleased, especially as this lordship was followed by the title and rights of "Grand Master of the Order of St John of Malta", while he could reward his mistress, *Anna Lopukhina*, for her beauty, with the title of "Grand Lady of the Order of St John of Malta".

By a new imperial decree of 1797, the Masonic lodges — which had already received permission — were forbidden to operate with the connivance of the Jesuits, and the ban was enforced with full severity.

But Paul did not succeed. Both the island of Malta and the benefits of its prestigious title were denied him.

A year after the island of Malta was taken by the English, Paul died, murdered by conspirators. The throne was now in the hands of his son *Alexander I*, who had been raised with great care by his grandmother Catherine.

His reign began quite well for a Freemason. The new ruler was a noble, philanthropic and liberal man, whose principles corresponded well with the Masonic point of view. He therefore looked with a rather lenient eye on the secret rise of Freemasonry in Russia, and it was not surprising that it was officially legalized again in 1810.

The movement was then revived and given new impetus. Lodges were established throughout the vast Russian Empire, even in Siberia. Within ten years, their number had risen to 31. Famous and well-known names in Russia can be found in the membership lists of the lodges, such as *Mikael Speransky, Benkendorff, Prince Ypsilanti, Prince Hohenlohe, Duke Alexander of Wür-*

temberg, the poet Kotzebue, etc., as well as a large number of top officers and administrators. One of the rules of the Grand Lodge at that time stated its purpose: "To promote human happiness by the practice of chastity, good works and religion, by faithful service to the sovereign and by submission to the strict observance of the laws of the land."

With its revival, the Masonic movement in Russia seemed outwardly successful. But at its roots remained its former weaknesses: dissension within and between lodges. Lodges operated under different systems, and it was difficult to coordinate their activities. Even now, Freemasonry could not move on a national basis because the influence of foreigners was quite strong.

In the beginning, Alexander — it is not known whether he was a Freemason himself — was quite favorable to the movement; indeed, he often used high-ranking Freemasons as advisors. This undoubtedly made it easy for him to familiarize himself with the various currents in Masonic circles and to discover their weaknesses. He therefore gradually became suspicious of them, especially since the attempts at revolution in Italy, Spain and Portugal at the same time were said to have been caused by Freemasons. Partly for the same reason, *Pope Pius VII* had also taken up the fight against Freemasonry, issuing a special proclamation of excommunication against it. Similarly, the Austrian statesman *Metternich*, with the Jesuits behind him, did everything in his power to discredit the Freemasons in the eyes of Alexander and to make them appear dangerous to the Empire.

Alexander, whose worldview had already become rather old-fashioned and reactionary, gradually matured in his decision to abolish the lodges throughout his empire. He was given a very welcome opportunity to do so when a secret society operating under the name of "Charity" — which in all respects had nothing to do with Freemasonry — was exposed for plotting against the Emperor's life. By decree of August 6, 1822, Alexander ordered all secret societies — including Masonic lodges — to cease to exist throughout the Russian Empire.

From that time on, there was no more Masonic activity in Russia. The current Russian rulers — the Bolsheviks — treated this movement in exactly the same way as their former imperialist predecessors. But once again the name "Freemason" appeared in Russian history, and in a rather shocking form. The change of regime led to a military rebellion by the so-called Decembrists, or Decemberists. This was bloodily defeated by Alexander's brother and successor, *Nicholas I.* It resulted in the hanging of 5 conspirators and the sentencing of several hundred of them to hard labor or to Siberia. The chronicles tell us that four of those hanged were Freemasons, among them Princes Sergei Trubetskoy and Kakhovsky.

The following year, a new imperial decree was issued, again prohibiting the operation of Masonic lodges in Russia — and, at the same time, in Finland. The measure was completely unnecessary, as there were no lodges in Russia at that time.

It is interesting to remember that Freemasonry was allowed to operate in Russia for only half a century. There is no doubt that it had a significant impact on the political and cultural conditions of the time. The history of Freemasonry puts many of the events of that period into context and sheds light on them. It also has a special significance for understanding contemporary circumstances.

Freemasonry is waiting to re-enter Russia. The fact that it failed there and could not take root on Russian soil was undoubtedly due to the level of civilization in that country at the time, when the Russian light, non-constructive character came to the fore. Moreover, it had not yet had the opportunity to become active on a national basis, which is a necessary condition for Masonic work. Foreign, alien elements were able to influence this movement and mix in their own aspirations and hobbies. This makes the image of Russian Freemasonry less than pleasant, almost sad.

But when Freemasonry is allowed to enter Russia again, it is to be hoped that it will have different conditions and opportunities than before. It will undoubtedly have the opportunity to take root on more national soil than before.

Then, too, it will be invincible.

IV

THE SOURCES USED IN THE USED IN THE PREPARATION OF THIS BOOK:

K.G. Leinberg: *Bidrag till Frimureriets i Finland historia; Svenska Litteratursjällskapets i Finland Förhandlingar och Uppsatser* (1906).

Viktor Lounasmaa: *Elämäni taipaleelta* (1910).

Aug. Horneffer: *Der Bund der Freimaurerei*, Jena (1913).

Heinr. Möller: *Die Alten Pflichten der Freimaurerei* (1913).

С. П. Мельгунова, Н. П. Сидорова, Масонство, 1915.

Paul Knak: *Kleiner Führer in die Geschichte und Organisation der Freimaurerei*, Berlin (1918).

Ernst Friedrichs: *Die Freimaurerei in Russland und Polen*, Berlin.

Ludvig Keller: *Die geiftigen Grundlagen der Freimaurerei und das offentliche Leben*, Berlin (1922).

Otto Philipp Neumann, *Freimaurertum*, Berlin (1922).

Ossian Lang: *History of Freemasonry in the State of New York* (1922).

Proceedings of the Grand Loge of Free and Accepted Masons of the State New-York (1922).

TRANSLATOR'S ADDITIONS
(not part of the original book)

The first 27 candidates who received degrees 1–3.

A. V. Solitander	Eero Jalas
K. Kivipohja	Hugo Rautapää
Alexander Frey	O. J. A. Viljanen
W. R. Wahlfors	Toivo Kaipio
V. M. J. Viljanen	Toivo K. Pajari
Gunnar Jaatinen	Samuli Sario
W. F. Risku	Aarno Jalas
K. N. Rantakari	A. H. Saastamoinen
K. A. Paloheimo	Jean Sibelius
Artturi Hellman	Sigurd Wettenhovi-Aspa
Aleksanteri Huuri	Leo Ehrnrooth
Ilmari Helenius	Hj. J. Procopé
Janne Kallio	Hugo Lindberg
A. H. Paloheimo	

During the meeting, the election of officers was held and the first Lodge, Suomi Loosi No. 1, was inaugurated and the officers installed. Axel Solitander was elected as the first Worshipful Master.

Deputy Grand Master Toivo H. Nekton and his officers at the inauguration of the Suomi Loosi No. 1 Temple in Helsinki, Unioninkatu 13, 24 November 1923.

Seated from left to right: *John P. Newton-Niskanen, Alfred Holmström, Toivo H. Nekton, Samuli Sario and Eero Jalas.*

Standing from left to right: *Viktor Willstedt, Wäinö Sola, Toivo Kontio, G.R. Nieminen, Carolus Lindberg, V.M.J. Viljanen, Axel Solitander, Jussi Tuokkola, Toivo Tainio, Y. Solitander, Jussi Tuokkola, Toivo Tainio, Y. Snellman, Toivo K. Pajari, Armas Ilmonen.*

★　★　★

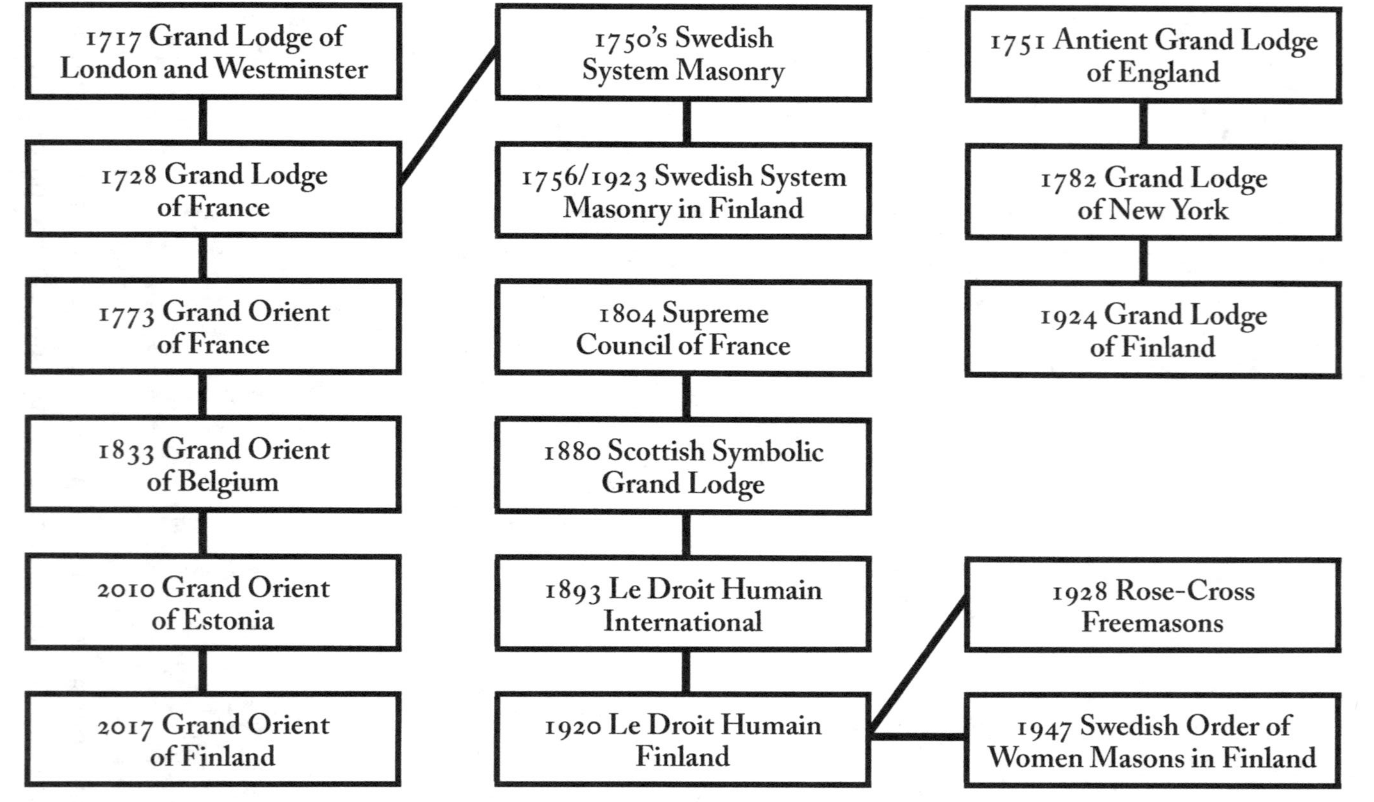

Origin chart of Masonic organisations in Finland 2024